MW00414632

THE QUOTABLE NEGAN

BLE NEGAN

**Warped Witticisms and Obscene Observations
from *The Walking Dead*'s Most Iconic Villain**

ROBERT KIRKMAN

SKYBOUND
BOOKS

ATRIA

New York London Toronto Sydney New Delhi

SKYBOUND BOOKS

ATRIA

An Imprint of Simon & Schuster, Inc.
1230 Avenue of the Americas
New York, NY 10020

First Skybound Books / Atria Books hardcover edition July 2018

SKYBOUND BOOKS / **ATRIA** B O O K S and colophon are trademarks of Simon & Schuster, Inc.

For information about special discounts for bulk purchases, please contact Simon & Schuster Special Sales at 1-866-506-1949 or business@simonandschuster.com.

The Simon & Schuster Speakers Bureau can bring authors to your live event. For more information or to book an event, contact the Simon & Schuster Speakers Bureau at 1-866-248-3049 or visit our website at www.simonspeakers.com.

Interior design by Jason Snyder

Manufactured in the United States of America

10 9 8 7 6 5 4 3 2 1

Library of Congress Cataloging-in-Publication Data is available.

ISBN 978-1-5011-8137-5
ISBN 978-1-5011-8138-2 (ebook)

To Lucille . . . for obvious reasons.

CONTENTS

Foreword by Robert Kirkman · ix

Intimidations and Insults · 1

A Way with (Swear) Words · 25

My Love! My Life! My Lucille! · 33

Everyone's a Fucking Comedian · 45

The Softer Side · 61

Loverboy or Loser? · 75

He Majored in Badassery;
Minored in Fucking Shit Up · 87

ACKNOWLEDGMENTS · 103

FOREWORD

I am Negan.

Or, really, I'm not. I'm really, really, *really* not. I swear I'm not—but some people who know me, well…they claim to see some similarities. For instance, sometimes I say weird shit the way Negan does. I'm not nearly as profane, and I'm certainly not as sadistic, but I've been prone to a few Neganisms from time to time.

Whenever I have exceptionally good news—which I'm fortunate enough to be able to report is somewhat often—I like to call up friends and say, "Do you have your shitting pants on?" as if to imply that people own special pants for shitting into upon hearing good news. I mean…it's just a funny thing to say. It makes me laugh.

Perhaps my most Negan-like trait (most people would say "flaw") is that I do and say a lot of weird things to entertain myself. I don't think most people are as committed to entertaining themselves as Negan and I are. I'll sometimes risk making my wife angry by saying something I don't mean simply because I know it'll be funny. What's up with that? I mean, I recognize how insane that is—and yet...

One time, to describe how like her mother my wife is, I said, "The apple doesn't fall far from the cunt." Now...Jesus...I know, I know. The thing is, for the most part, I don't use that word at all. I certainly don't use it in the company of my wife, whom I've been with for nearly twenty years—and I *definitely* would never use it to describe my mother-in-law, who is a fantastic person. But the thing is...

...I thought it would be funny.

And it *was*. My wife, as I recall, was so stunned by what I'd said that she wasn't mad at all; she just chuckled and moved on. She's an awesome lady, and I mean that. I'm not just saying that because I think she's going to read this. I'm fairly certain she never will; and if she does, the fact that I wrote this for public consumption would probably make her so angry that she wouldn't speak to me for a week. Which is something her mother does.

(My wife doesn't really do that; I just thought it would be a funny thing to write.)

Anyway, the point is . . . fuck. Maybe I'm more like Negan than I'd care to admit.

I am, at my core, a well-meaning person, and I care about other people's feelings. While I've never bashed anyone's brains in with a baseball bat or actually caused any physical harm to another person in any way, I *have* ruined my fair share of people's days by saying something stupid or poking fun at someone or ridiculing someone a little too much, past the point of their being in on the joke—and then I keep going.

It's a sickness.

I have plenty of friends, and they seem to really like me, but I'm what can best be described as an acquired taste.

And so is Negan. He's a very divisive character who incited many complaints when he was introduced in the comic books and the television show. Honestly, the fact that he's so divisive is one of the reasons I like him so much. I mean, one of the things that makes *The Walking Dead* so popular is that it takes things very seriously. Dead people are up and walking around, sure, but aside from that (and the occasional bazooka on the TV show), things are treated as though they're very real and grounded. So, after years of high drama and lots of crying and very solemn speeches, this wisecracking, constantly cursing lunatic barges in, says a *ton* of stupid stuff, and then kills a beloved character with a baseball bat (or two, if you're talking about the show). That's going to be more than a little jarring for most people. You can see how that seemed downright out of place for some.

Make no mistake: Negan is one of the most popular characters to ever appear in *The Walking Dead*...but not for everyone.

Some people *hate* Negan, some people *love* him, and others

love to hate him. I have to be completely honest: I love the guy. I love him so much that I've intended to kill him twice in the comic series, and both times I've changed my mind.

The first time was when he was first introduced. Negan was only ever supposed to be in six issues of the comic series. He was going to kill Glenn, and then a few short issues later Rick was going to kill him and deliver his severed head to Maggie as a gift. And she was going to...I don't know, bury the head? Set it on fire? Impale it on a spike? I don't know what you do with the head of the man who killed your husband (and I hope I never have to find out). I hadn't worked it all out. Negan was to have pushed the characters into such a dark place that our beloved hero, Rick Grimes, would present his severed head to our beloved heroine, Maggie, and she would respond by saying "Thank you" with heartfelt sincerity.

But damn it—Negan was just too entertaining to me.

The second time, which I'm exclusively revealing here, was much more recent. In issue #174, Maggie goes to kill Negan, who by this point in the story is living alone in exile, a miserable, lonely shell of the man he once was. In the published comic, she sees how broken he is and realizes that it's a greater punishment to leave him alive, more or less—so despite his begging her to kill him, she leaves without doing him in. As the script was originally written, though, after Negan begs Maggie to kill him, Maggie kind of impulsively shoots him in the head. The gun goes off, and she instantly regrets it. She hadn't intended to shoot him in that moment, but something inside her makes her pull the trigger. She's upset and leaves him dead in his lonely little house. I sent this script to series artist Charlie Adlard, and had he just drawn it, that's what would have happened. But Charlie emailed me to say how much he liked the idea of a reformed Negan. He didn't ask me to change the story, but said it bummed him out to lose Negan this way.

That's all it took.

As soon as he said that, I immediately came up with a new ending to that issue that was not only better but also had Negan

remain alive, to do . . . who knows what in upcoming issues. I certainly won't spoil that here.

To me, the pinnacle of this entire series is a panel in issue #105 in which Negan says, "I'm just fucking with you! A baseball bat doesn't have a pussy!" I just love that. It's the most insane panel that's ever appeared in the comic. Out of context, it's also the weirdest moment in the book. If you took that single panel back in time to show me when I was working on issue #20, I would be convinced that I'd lost my mind. I would argue that that panel didn't belong in *The Walking Dead*—but I would be wrong. So, so wrong.

The fact that a panel like that is allowed to exist is a testament to the series' having achieved the kind of evolution I aspire to accomplish with each individual character. *The Walking Dead* has grown and changed over time; it's the same book, but it's vastly different. I feel like that's a huge success. You don't last fifteen years (and counting) by telling the same story over and over again without changing things up.

And look—Negan has grown in popularity to the point that there's a nifty little book collecting many of the horrible things I've made him say over the years. Most of you must love this guy. I mean, how could you not with Jeffrey Dean Morgan bringing him to life on sixteen Sunday nights a year? That face could make you love the devil himself, right?

Still, I'm willing to admit that it's possible Negan is a character who shouldn't have appeared in the series, and I'm just keeping him in to make me laugh. I've done far worse for a laugh, that's for sure.

ROBERT KIRKMAN
Backwoods, CA
March 2018

INTIMIDATIONS
and INSULTS

Negan is perhaps best known for his sharp tongue, acerbic commentary, and viciously quick wit. He can threaten you with creative methods for your demise or cut you down to size with a masterful insult. Have a look at some of the bastard's best burns and most creative terrorizations.

Oh, baby... We pissing our pants yet? Oh, boy—do I have a feeling we're getting *close*. It's going to be pee pee pants city here *real* soon. Which one of you pricks is the leader?

—ISSUE #100

Anyone moves... at all... cut the boy's other fucking eye out and feed it to the girl. You can breathe... You can blink... You can cry... You're *all* going to be doing that.

—ISSUE #100

You see, Rick. Whatever you do...no matter fucking what...you *do not* mess with the New World Order. The New World Order is this, and it's *very* simple, so even if you're fucking stupid...which you may very well be...you can understand it. Ready? Here goes...pay attention.

Give me your shit or I will kill you.

You work for me now, you have shit—you give it to me. *That's* your job. I know it's a mighty fucking big, nasty pill to swallow, but swallow it you most certainly motherfucking will. You ruled the roost, you built something, you thought you were safe, I get it... But the word is out, you are not safe...not even fucking close. In fact, you're *fucked*. And even *more* fucked if you don't fucking give me what I want.

—ISSUE #100

3

Things have changed, Rick. Whatever you had going for you—that's over. You answer to *me*. You provide for *me*. You *belong* to *me*. Welcome to a brand new beginning, you sorry fucks. We'll come for your first offering in *one week*. Until then...

—ISSUE #100

Pardon me, young man, and fucking excuse the shit out of my goddamn French...but did you just *threaten* me? That sounded like a threat, but I like to be *damn sure* when it comes to these kinds of things.

—ISSUE #103

In case you haven't caught on...I just slid my dick down your throat...and you thanked me for it.

—ISSUE #103

You know what, *stop.* I can't go on like this. It's like talking to a fucking birthday present. Take that shit off your face—I gotta see what Grandma got me....Fucking Christ, man! No wonder you cover that shit up. You look disgusting. Have you *seen* it?! I mean—have you looked in a mirror? I wouldn't blame you if you hadn't. It's fucking *gross*. I can see your fucking eye socket—your goddamn skull is exposed. Now I want to touch it. Can I touch it?

—ISSUE #105

Everyone toes the line because I provide them a service. I keep them safe. We're the *Saviors*, not the *kill-your-friends-so-you-don't-fucking-like-us-at-alls.*

Are we going to kill your friends if you don't cooperate?! *Absolutely.* I'm pretty sure I've established that.

—ISSUE #107

In case you haven't noticed...you're fucking *fucked*, you stupid fucker.

—ISSUE #112

We're the *big swinging dick* of this world—have been for a long fucking time...but it seems people are forgetting that. So now our big dick is going to swing harder...and faster, until we take off like a *motherfucking helicopter* and blow all these motherfuckers away.

We're going to *war*.

—ISSUE #114

I've considered your kind offer...and I'm thinking of an answer somewhere between *no motherfucking way* and *go fucking fuck yourself*!

—ISSUE #116

I hope you have your shitting pants on.

Your *shitting pants.* I hope you're wearing them right now...because you're about to shit your fucking pants.

—ISSUE #116

Most of all—*don't fucking die!* I better not lose one man to these undead fucks, you fuckers! You fucking die and I will fuck you up!

—ISSUE #117

You brought this on yourself, Rick! I was willing to work with you...all you had to do was follow the fucking rules. Now I see you've got to fucking go. *Scorched fucking Earth, you dick!*

—ISSUE #120

If that still doesn't fucking do it...I'll start cutting pieces off...I see...I see me starting with the piece of you that is most valued...and yet losing it wouldn't prevent you from doing your work. That's right, you fat fuck—it's your shriveled up little dick.

That's the path that lies ahead for you. It's set in stone...the only thing you can do to stop it...is cooperate. And I really fucking hope you do, because while Lucille is always thirsty...I don't want to get dirty, I don't want to have to deal with the mess...and I really don't want to have to cut your dick off.

But I do things I don't want to do all the fucking time.

—ISSUE #121

Hello? Anybody home?! White flag... I come in peace! To accept your *peaceful surrender!*

I think technically waving the white flag means *I'm surrendering*... but let's not be stupid, okay? You fuckers got your *asses* handed to you with a side order of *my dick up those asses.* Heh. So... let's talk. I'm sure you don't want to fight anymore, so let's not fucking fight. Let's be fuck buddies again and stop all this fighting. Let's move from one *"F"* to the other *"F,"* my *favorite "F."* Let's *end* this goddamn war.

—ISSUE #125

This time of day reminds me of the worst part of being here... and the *best.* The fact that I have to shit in a bucket... and the fact that *you're* the one cleaning out my shit bucket.

—ISSUE #129

Look at Grandpa Grimes, sluggishly going for his gun. How high can you even lift that thing? Enough to reach my face, or will you be going for a gut shot? Are you sure your arm is strong enough? It's been doing a lot of *cane* work these days, right? That make it stronger or wear it out? I guess we'll find out, right?

Really, Papaw? Are you fucking kidding me with this shit? Do you have any fucking idea how easily I could have fucked you up just now? I could have you bent over those stairs right now, driving my fist right up into your asshole. You'd be my fucking Rick puppet. I could punch your balloon knot until it looks like a turkey's ass on Thanksgiving.

—ISSUE #141

I expect you to be *suspicious as fuck* and run around checking this whole goddamn fucking town for fucking booby traps and shit. *How* long have I been free? Did I knock a fucking hole in the wall around this place? Did I mess with the wires in your basement so your home will burn down tonight with you in it? Did I bring out my perfectly *normal-sized wiener* and fuck orgasms into your girl Andrea until she ordered a T-shirt from the *Negan's Cock Fan Club?!*

—ISSUE #141

Point me in the right direction, and shut the fuck up. I'm the one calling the shots now. Fall in line or fall down a fucking well.

—ISSUE #153

I'm not going to get through this without fucking killing you, am I? And that's how little motherfucking respect I have for you, kid. I'm asking that . . . out loud . . . right the fuck in front of you. Am I going to have to kill you?

—ISSUE #153

Oh, don't be such a crybaby. The fucking world ended. *Everyone's* mother is dead. You pussy. Besides . . . we're on our way to *talk* to the people who cut your mom's head off . . . have some motherfucking perspective.

—ISSUE #153

I'm not a fucking idiot. I can fucking count and I can count *ten* of you. The rest are undead fucks...and while I appreciate you holding those stupid fucks at bay, I'd bet my *handsomest nut* only *two* of you can actually fight. I'm not going to win a full-blown fight, especially with you...*Frowny McTwoKnives* jumping in. But I'm goddamn motherfucking sure as fucking *fuck* that I'll kill at least three of you smelly piss bowls before you get me. Maybe I only get a good stab in a few of you—you die later.

—ISSUE #154

Limp dick giant fuck. Fuck you, Softy McDickface...

—ISSUE #156

Tear my pants off, prick. See what I got. I'll knock your fucking teeth out with my swinging dick!

—ISSUE #156

You tell me I have to crush a field of babies to keep breathing? Sure. You say people who rely on me aren't going to live unless I turn someone's head into a bowl of gravy? I'm there. I don't feel bad about it. I don't think about it. It just *is what it is.* It's *survival.*

—ISSUE #156

Yeah. That's right. It's *me*. Now get the fuck off the ground...

So I can put you *in* it...like...in a coffin. Because you'll be *fucking dead*...after I fucking kill you, you fucking asshole.

—ISSUE #158

News at fucking eleven. Ask me if I give a fuck.

—ISSUE #161

Let's see some killing, you timid fucks! These skulls aren't going to pierce themselves. Suck your nuts up into your crotch and put your fucking *backs* into it!

—ISSUE #163

Fine, play the part of the uptight guy at the dick-sucking contest and keep your fucking mouth shut. See if I care. Best to be quiet so these dead fucks out here will lose interest in us and start following the other dumb fucks when they walk past going down the road.

—ISSUE #164

Think about those days. Things worked on a points system. Doing deeds and performing tasks got you points, and you could use those points to get goods and supplies...food and shit... *it was great!* Where'd we get that stuff? People fucking *brought* it to us... and they gave it to us. Did they do that because they loved us? *Hell fucking fuck no!* They fucking *hated* us. *Me most of all.*

But they also fucking *feared* us...
and again, *me most of all.*

—ISSUE #168

17

You of *all fucking people* want to go back to the way things *were?!* I cooked the side of your *fucking face* for fuck's sake, you fucking fucked up fuck! You want to go back to *that?!* To fucking *face-cooking* when it was *your fucking face?!*

Jesus, Mark . . . you're a special kind of sheep, aren't you? Watch out for this one, everyone. *Fuck.*

—ISSUE #168

Eat knife, you *smelly fucking fuck!*

Try to fucking eat *me*? You get piping hot *buttered blade* instead—fresh from *Mama Negan's* Motherfucking Death Kitchen of Death!

—ISSUE #170

You pull your pud that slow, fuckwit?! *Game point!*

If I had a wrist that weak, I'd need *three*
pictures of your mom to blow my load. Now
which one of you little pricks is next?

—HERE'S NEGAN!

Put your hands in front of your tummies, I don't want
the raging hard-ons this news is about to give you to
cause any gut punches. Paul, looks like you could use a
good hard-on. Don't let them go to waste at your age!

—HERE'S NEGAN!

Things sneaking up on me in the dark
are either dead or about to be...

—HERE'S NEGAN!

It's almost dark, stranger. You leading me to a trap?
I must warn you, I'm a bad motherfucker who will
split your skull the fuck in half if you cross me.

—HERE'S NEGAN!

You guys look like you're on a nonstop bullet train to pee
pee pants city. Like you can't even process... you can't.

—HERE'S NEGAN!

Look at this *big-balled motherfucker* right here. I like that, that's useful, so here's what I'd say, **Big Balls**.

Fall *the fuck* in line or I'll crawl up that pee hole of yours, get really deep inside so I can really get a message to those big balls without anything getting lost in translation.

And I'll say—Big Balls, I know you think you're king shit of fuck mountain and you're not accustomed to taking shit from anyone, but things are *different* now because—*Here's Negan!*

—HERE'S NEGAN!

FASTER, NEGAN!

AS IF THERE WAS ANY DOUBT, Negan most definitely backs up these words with dirty deeds and cold-blooded murder. Here's a look at his kill count—which is impressive, to say the least.

Total Kills:

42

KILL! KILL! KILL!

Walkers:
34

Issue #103: **2**

Issue #117: **4**

Issue #156: **1**

Issue #158: **2**

Issue #163: **3**

Issue #165: **4**

Issue #166: **2**

Issue #170: **2**

Here's Negan!: **14**

Humans:
6

Glenn (Issue #100)

Spencer (Issue #111)

David (Issue #117)

Brandon (Issue #153)

Alpha (Issue #156)

Unnamed Rival (*Here's Negan!*)

Animals:
2

Dog (Issue #174)

Rabbit (*Here's Negan!*)

DEADLIEST EPISODES:
Issue #117 (**4 walkers** + **David**) and *Here's Negan!* (**14 walkers**, an unnamed **rival**, and one sweet little **bunny rabbit**)

A WAY WITH (SWEAR) WORDS

With its nearly infinite variations, visceral imagery, and pleasing utterance, "fuck" is far and away Negan's favorite word in the English language. We present for you a small sampling of Negan's creative usage of "fuck." One could call this his Greatest Fucking Hits...

So I'm now going to beat the *holy fuck fucking fuckedy fuck* out of one of you...

—ISSUE #100

[S]hit fuck, kid—lighten up.

—ISSUE #100

[I]t's motherfucking cocksucking magnificent! *Wow!*

—ISSUE #103

Stand the fuck up, you fucking fucker.

—ISSUE #107

Still—here I am, friendly as a fuckless
fuck on free fuck day.

—ISSUE #107

That's out-fucking-rageous.

—ISSUE #111

[Y]ou're fucking *fucked,* you stupid fucker.

—ISSUE #112

Motherfucking motherfuckers.

—ISSUE #114

*Motherfucking dick suck cunt fucking fuck
fuckity fuck fucker fucking fuck fuckers!*

—ISSUE #117

Fuck. Fuck. Fuck. Fuck.

—ISSUE #125

Fucking fuck no!

—ISSUE #159

Any-fuck-fucking-fuckity-way...

—ISSUE #164

Okay, Jesus fucking Christ!

—ISSUE #165

Jack-*mother-fucking*-pot!

—ISSUE #174

Fuck you, fucking expired fucking canned
fucking food! Fuckity fucking *fuck!*

—ISSUE #174

Well, would you fucking fuck fuckity look at that?

—ISSUE #174

Fucking fuck fuckity fuck!!

—HERE'S NEGAN!

A STATISTICAL ANALYSIS OF A FILTHY MOUTH

IN THE NAME OF SCIENCE, we broke down every single "fuck" ever uttered by Negan in the comics. We knew he was a prolific blasphemer but, frankly, we were astonished by the final count...

Total Fucks Given: 792

Fuck(s):
222

Fucking:
474

Fucked:
18

Fuckers:
15

Motherfuck(ing):	33
Motherfucker(s):	15
Fuckidy/Fuckity:	5
Fuck You:	4
Fucked Up:	1
Fuckable:	1
Absofuckinglutely:	1
Fuckhead:	1
Fuckless:	1
Fuckwit:	1

MY LOVE! MY LIFE! MY LUCILLE!

Every good villain (or hero, for that matter) needs an iconic weapon and an intense relationship with that particular piece of hardware. Negan's relationship with Lucille is definitely intense. "Fucking weird" might be another way to put it...

So I'm now going to beat the *holy fuck fucking fuckedy fuck* out of one you with my bat. Who I call "Lucille." Lucille has *barbed wire* wrapped around the end of her. It's fucking *awesome.* So, it's really just a matter of picking which one of you gets the honor.

—ISSUE #100

You bunch of pussies... I'm just getting started. Lucille is *thirsty.*

—ISSUE #100

You carried her all the way up here for me? Were you gentle? Were you *kind?* Did you treat her like a lady? Did you eat her *pussy* like a lady?

I'm just *fucking* with you! A baseball bat doesn't have a *pussy!* Now get the fuck out of here.

—ISSUE #105

You even made me drop Lucille. You have any fucking clue how much she *hates* being on the ground? She's like an American flag that way. You just don't let it happen—it's disrespectful.

—ISSUE #107

I take *no* joy in those [evil] deeds. *Lucille* on the other hand . . . thankfully she's *not* in charge.

—ISSUE #107

You know Lucille is always *D.T.F.!*

—ISSUE #113

You may think this is an inanimate object. An inconsequential piece of wood wrapped carefully with barbed wire...not something to be *cherished.* And you'd be *dead fucking wrong.* This is a lady...But at times, yeah...she ain't so nice...Truth is...Lucille is a *bitch.* But she's *my* bitch. This bitch has saved my life more times than I can remember.

She's the only bitch I've ever *truly* loved. If I could...I'd *fuck* her. And yes...that means in my most private of moments I've probably rubbed my dick against her. I'm not ashamed to admit it.

—ISSUE #113

Would that make you jealous? I'm sure it fucking would. You're a jealous bitch, aren't you? You're jealous of those grenades, right? You want in on the action . . . you want to get *dirty*, don't you?

I can't blame you—sitting on the outside, hearing the screams behind those walls, watching the fires burn . . . it's like being a double amputee at a peep show. I'm just sitting here trying to figure out how to suck my own dick.

—ISSUE #120

Now look at this! The new and improved, better than before, all awesome and abso-fucking-lutely *deadly* Lucille. I don't have to crush your head or pound your face through the back of your skull with her anymore. The slightest touch from Lucille...just a kiss...and she's left her mark.

—ISSUE #122

This is my *Excalibur!* My flashing invincibility star! My can of *motherfucking spinach!* You are fucking *fucked,* Jolly Green!

—ISSUE #159

Nooooooooo!

You! You fucking *broke* her!

You broke Lucille!! Fuck! *No!*

—ISSUE #160

Lucille.

I missed you so much. I know I'm pathetic.
I know you're just splintered pieces of
wood. But you're—You're all I have . . .

—ISSUE #170

You're not a fucking baseball bat. I'm talking to you like a crazy person, but you're my dead wife...Lucille. Not the baseball bat I named after you. That was just a fucking baseball bat. I didn't love it. Not *really*. I can replace the bat...That's not replacing *you*. *It's not.*

—ISSUE #174

I know [the barbed wire] is probably restricting and tight now, but you will get used to it, dear. I fucking *promise* the fuck out of that. Pretty soon it'll be like a second skin...you'd feel naked without it, but you'll never fucking be without it because it's a fucking part of you. Fuck *yes*, it is.

—ISSUE #174

Nice *bat.*

—HERE'S NEGAN!

This is Lucille. Instead of watching you sorry fucks die like I have so many other weak motherfuckers along the way...I have a new idea. I'll let Lucille protect you, too.

Stand with me...and anyone who tries to hurt us... anyone who gets in our way...will end up like him.

—HERE'S NEGAN!

LUCILLE

Negan!:
e origins
, as well
reation
aviors.

Issue #103:
Negan briefly gives
Lucille to Rick while
visiting the compound.

Issue #126:
Lucille is stolen
by Dwight.

Issue #100:
Negan introduces
Lucille to the world…
via Glenn's head.

Issue #113:
Carl damages
Lucille's tip when
shooting at Negan

TIMELINE

Issue #150:
Appearance;
still in Dwight's
possession.

Issue #159:
But the reunion is
short-lived: Lucille
breaks just a few
pages later.

Issue #174:
A new bat makes a
brief appearance...
but is tossed into the
fire shortly after.

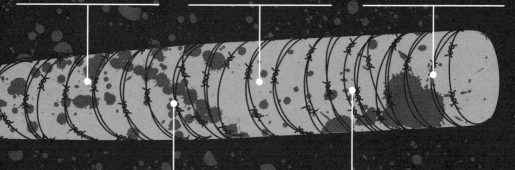

Issue #159:
Negan and Lucille
are reunited!
Sweet fuckity fuck!

Issue #162:
It is revealed that Negan
had named Lucille
after his late wife.

EVERYONE'S A FUCKING COMEDIAN

It's not all doom and gloom and skull-bashin' with Negan, no sir. His sense of humor might be macabre as fuck, but a man has to find the time and space for a little levity if he wants to survive. Especially at the end of the world.

Heh...Lucille is a vampire bat.

What? Was the joke *that* bad?

—ISSUE #100

I gave you your son back...without harming
so much as one exposed bone on his head.
Heh. I said "exposed bone" instead of "hair."
That's not even getting a chuckle? Well, *I*
thought it was funny, you stoic piece of shit.

—ISSUE #107

You ever hear the one about the stupid fuck named Rick who fucking thought he knew shit but didn't know shit and got himself fucking killed? It was about *you.* You got that, right?

—ISSUE #112

I really wanted to see that little fucker tumble down. See what all the king's horses and all the king's men could do with the pieces. Humpty Dumpty joke. Why the fuck would anyone expect a *horse* to be able to put an *egg* back together? It's like, "The men and the horses can't do it—this guy's fucked!"

Wouldn't they call in the *women?* They have smaller fingers. That rhyme makes no goddamn sense.

—ISSUE #113

My dick is so hard right now I could crack steel. I should wrap it in barbed wire and call it *Lucille Two.*

—ISSUE #120

I have eyes...so *fuck yes* I know what you are. People wearing skin suits to mask themselves from the dead. Or is this like a fucking Looney Tunes thing and there's another zipper under the human skin and you're dogs inside? Are you guys like *living* Russian nesting dolls?

—ISSUE #154

[D]o I get to pick my own skin suit later? I'm going to need one with a . . . *generous* crotch area . . . on account of my thick, meaty dick. You guys put zippers in there? Some kind of button?

I can't undo a bunch of buttons to take a piss, y'know?

—ISSUE #154

I've been told I don't always make the best first impressions. But I grow on people. I'm a *grower*, not a *show-er* . . . Is that what that phrase refers to? First impressions?

—ISSUE #155

Seriously. I get *zero* fucking weapons here?

I'm about as useful as a fingerless eunuch during Fuck Fest February! Someone *give me a gun!*

—ISSUE #158

Let's play rock, paper, knives, bat.

Bat. *Smashes.* Knives.

—ISSUE #159

Oh, baby! It's like I'm the last man on Earth, tasked with getting *all* the women pregnant! But instead of rapidly putting my penis into a million vaginas—I'm pushing this knife into rotted fucking skulls!

Judge all you want, Rick—*this is thrilling!*

—ISSUE #165

Seriously, this is *so fun*. It's like carving a pumpkin! It's more fun than carving a pumpkin—*because pumpkins aren't human fucking heads!*

—ISSUE #165

Pork and fucking beans. Am I right? I mean, were it up to me, I'd take every single can and nothing else...Just eat that shit until I popped and fucking died. I'd die a happy man, pork and beans leaking out of every hole, old and new.

The new hole is from where I popped, Dwight.

—ISSUE #169

Listen here, sunflower—you are fucking *gorgeous!* Don't let anyone tell you any different. Least of all this stupid motherfucking grass. Grass don't know shit. Fuck you, grass.

Holy shit...look at you. Looks like we got something in motherfucking common, sunflower. We've both got long, *thick* roots! You think that's a regional thing? Root being a word for dick?

Then again, what *isn't* a word for dick?

Vagina really is the only one that doesn't work...and yet, if people said it enough...it would eventually catch on.

I'd like to sling my vagina up in that vagina. Heh.

—ISSUE #174

I traded in nice for funny a long time ago. You'd be surprised how much better it works. Nice is boring. Nice has never led to fucking in the history of anything, ever. Funny fucks all day and night.

—HERE'S NEGAN!

Maybe you'll be taking my beating in return. I mean, I'll give you a beating, not that you'll be...That was supposed to sound fucking clever and it...Let me start over. I haven't spoken out loud in a few weeks.

—HERE'S NEGAN!

I've never fired a gun in my life. Feels like I've got a ten-foot dick made of giant dicks that ejaculate dicks. Seriously. Guns are the shit.

—HERE'S NEGAN!

Overcompensation? Sports cars and guns... all for guys with little dicks, right? *Horse shit.* My dick fires warm, pearly snot wads... this phallic majesty ejaculates hot fucking *death* into whatever I point it at. How can *any* dick compare to that?

—HERE'S NEGAN!

You know...you're right. That is mighty handy. It's like a condom you can wash out and use again...or really...like anything reusable. Don't know why I had to mention the condom. Just trying to be crass.

—HERE'S NEGAN!

I was a *bad motherfucker.* And by bad motherfucker, I mean gym teacher. You care for the kids, bark orders at them to keep them from getting fat...they may cry a little, but it's for their own fucking good, y'know?

—HERE'S NEGAN!

'TIS BUT A

WHEN HE'S NOT INSULTING SOMEONE, making a lewd joke, or bashing in some unfortunate walker's skull, Negan is busy getting his ass kicked. Take a look at the punishment endured by this consummate badass and walk away with a newfound appreciation for the man. Dude can certainly take a punch...

Damage Report

PUNCH/ SLAP:	KNEE/ KICK:	CHARGE/ TACKLE:	KNIFEBUTT/ GUNBUTT:	CHOKE HOLD:
4	2	2	2	2

HEADBUTT:	LUCILLE:	BITE:	BARBED WIRE:
1	1	1	1

SCRATCH

Who's Dealing the Damage?

RICK:

7

(headbutt, knee, charge/tackle x2, bite, knife slash, punch)

JESUS:

3

(Lucille, punch, choke hold)

ALPHA:

1

(punch)

BETA:

4

(choke hold, knifebutt, kick, gunbutt)

OLIVIA:

1

(slap)

UNNAMED RIVAL:

1

(push into barbed wire)

Target Areas

HEAD:

11

TORSO:

4

ARMS/LEGS:

2

THE SOFTER SIDE

Beneath Negan's tough-as-nails exterior
is another, super-impenetrable layer
of crass snark and crude euphemisms.
But if you can get through that,
there are some surprising nuggets
of humanity hidden among the dick
jokes, feces, and dried blood.

I understand our relationship started with me beating the holy fucking fuck out of your friend's head. The gravity of that event is not fucking lost on me. Let me assure you of that. I do not believe we will ever share a meal together and tell each other our deepest fucking darkest secrets. That said, goddamn it...I do feel like I have bent over *fucking backwards* in my attempts to show you just how reasonable I can be.

—ISSUE #112

You have no fucking idea how much I used to like that boy. Never had a kid of my own. When I saw him...got to know him, I thought...if I ever did have a fucking kid...I'd want a fucking kid like this fucking kid. Kid had huge fucking balls. *Huge.*

—ISSUE #113

Cheer up. She went quick. Probably
didn't feel a goddamn thing.

Of course, you always hear "my life flashed before my
eyes," and I've always said that in times of stress,
people perceive time differently. Like...things move
slower. So maybe even when the death is quick
you do feel something. Maybe that final painful
moment plays out for what seems like hours.

—ISSUE #114

I want you to know, I really do appreciate our
little talks. It...really breaks up my days.
Helps me...mark time. I think they're good
for you, too, having someone to talk to...

After all this time...all these talks...the things
we've shared. Do you still want to *kill* me?

—ISSUE #127

If your *instinct* is to hurt another person...to get pleasure from their pain...then you're a fucking *monster* and need to be put the fuck down. I've done *unspeakable* things...but I've *always* had a reason. It's *always* been for *a greater good.* Never for pleasure...

—ISSUE #156

I, um...I lost someone...*very* close to me. It was right before all this happened.

One day they were there...and then it all just fell apart. *They died.*

And it *broke* me. I don't *feel* anymore. I don't feel sad... I don't feel scared...I don't feel happy. I'm just...here.

That's *my* strength. That's why I'm *alive.*

—ISSUE #156

I never got to bury you before. I know this isn't the same... I'm sorry you were never *truly* put to rest. I'm hoping... this is the next best thing. This is the closest I can get. I hope you're at peace. I hope you... I hope you're in heaven, and you fell in love with someone who treats you better than I ever did, and that they're fucking your brains out and then fucking your brains back in after that on a daily basis.

I'll always miss you, Lucille.

I'm sorry I named a stupid fucking baseball bat after you.

—ISSUE #162

Worst thing I ever did was leave my wife to rot.

I couldn't do it, had someone else put her down. And *why?* I had some kind of compulsion at the time—the dead need to stay dead...like she was in *agony* or some shit...some kind of perversion of who she was...an *abomination.* Where did that come from? I had no—*still have no fucking clue* what it's like to be one of these undying fucks. Everything could taste like *pumpkin pie,* and it could be like a *never-ending* Neil Young concert in your head for all I know. Fucking *light shows* and shit.

But *no,* she was put down, and I didn't even see it. I even stayed in the area for weeks...never went back to do the right thing. I just...I couldn't *see* her like that again. I couldn't put her in the ground— put her to rest. She's a pile of dry bones rotting on a fucking floor...my wife...*because of me.*

—ISSUE #164

The fact that Rick will let you quietly do that...without lifting a fucking finger toward punishing you for rolling up guns-a-blazing to fuck his shit up, should *prove* to you what kind of guy he is. And if that ain't enough... fucking *wait*. Sit back in that factory I made livable for you and wait around until you need *help* with something... *and you most certainly fucking will*...

And ask Rick for that fucking help. Then watch him as he *politely provides* that help. *Then*... when he turns around and asks you for help...

You fucking help him.

Because that's what this is all about. Not control, not who's the boss, not whose dick is fucking longer and thicker and straighter and... it's about *helping each other. That's it.*

—ISSUE #168

I know you weren't much into flowers when you were alive... but then again, people change after the end of the world. Maybe if you'd lived... you'd have grown to appreciate a little *beauty* in this ugly world. Besides... there's not a whole hell of a lot to do these days.

And frankly, there's not much I can do to honor you... and let you know I'm thinking about you... other than this. I'm always thinking about you, Lucille. I want you to know that.

—ISSUE #174

Maggie... It's a *luxury* in this world to live long enough to regret the things you've done... to have a quiet enough moment to allow the memory of your actions to *horrify* you.

—ISSUE #174

My Lucille was dead...pretty much everyone anybody loved was *probably dead*...but if Glenn was *your* Lucille...Well, that's a pain I'm *all* too familiar with.

[K]ill me. I deserve it. Go ahead. *Do it.*

That would be poetic symmetry...*Painful* for me... but I respect it. I understand all too well how *satisfying* that would probably be...use the bat if you want.

Do it.

I can't live like this. I can't be alone. I can't...This is what I *deserve.* Pull the trigger, Maggie. *Do it! Please.*

Picture Glenn's face. Remember *that?!* Remember what I did? *That's* who I am! That's what I'm capable of. I could do that again.

I want this. *Please.* I want it all to end. I'm ready for this to be over! I *want* you to kill me. Will you *please* just kill me?!

—ISSUE #174

It's time I told you about *Lucille.*

Lucille meant *everything* to me. I didn't even
know it at the time. Not all the time, at least.
There were moments, but for the most part...*I
was a piece of shit.* It wasn't until she was *gone*
that I really knew what she meant to me.

—*HERE'S NEGAN!*

I learned something . . . being around those people, watching them die, one after another . . . because they were too weak . . . too scared . . . too mother . . . fucking . . . sad.

And me? Well . . . I felt *nothing.* Not for them. Not for myself. Not for anyone.

I wasn't scared. I wasn't sad. I wasn't angry . . . Well, sometimes I was angry. Sometimes I was *furious.* But for the most part . . . nothing. And it took me a long time to realize *why.*

It was *Lucille.*

She protected me. She placed me in a bubble where nothing got to me . . . made me *stronger.* Helped me survive.

—HERE'S NEGAN!

BUT WAIT, HE'S SUPPOSED TO BE A BAD MOTHER FUCKER!

WHEN YOU'RE DONE getting all misty-eyed at Negan's emotional, sensitive side, pull your peepers over to this list of Negan's favorite methods of murder. Back on task, people.

LUCILLE:

17

BIG FUCKIN' KNIFE:

16

RIFLE:

4

HANDGUN:

2

FIRE EXTINGUISHER TO THE HEAD:

2

IMMOLATION:

1

LOVERBOY OR LOSER?

Though he's about as subtle as a bat to the face, Negan thinks he has a way with the ladies. That way is the *absolutely wrong fucking way*, but it seems to work for him and is at least entertaining for the rest of us...

Okay, boys, let's get this shit unloaded and inside. Gonna be dark soon, and I want to be tucked in and catching some Zs with ample time to throw the wood in *at least* a couple of wives. You know what I'm saying?

I'm saying I'm going to fuck some of my girls tonight.

Get it?

—ISSUE #103

Wives? Yeah. I always wanted to be able to fuck a whole bunch of women—so why settle down with just one? I see no reason to follow the old *boring* rules. Let's make life *better*. Why not?

—ISSUE #105

When I choose a new wife, the process is completely voluntary. It's an honor to be with me, to no longer have to earn points to trade for goods and services. But it comes with a *price*...total devotion...and that can sometimes be a hard pill for others to swallow.

But swallow it they must...or it's the *iron* for you.

—ISSUE #105

Now if you'll excuse me, I'm going to go ping-pong my dick all over these titties.

—ISSUE #108

As much as I love violence...I absolutely fucking hate sexual violence. It's...unseemly.

—ISSUE #112

The fastest way to a man's heart is through his vagina.

A lot of people say it's the stomach. That's the saying . . . but that's fucking *stupid.*

All men like to eat, sure. But do *all* men place that much importance on their next meal? You cook a mean meatloaf and so you've fucking *got* them wrapped around your little fucking finger? No goddamn way.

Men love to *fuck.* All men. Every goddamn one of them. Young, old, fat, thin, smart, dumb, alive, dead . . . *all men.* After a while, a certain kind of man . . . men like Rick Grimes, they find one vagina they *really* enjoy being inside. That becomes *their vagina.*

You fuck with that vagina . . . *you can crush a man's heart.*

—ISSUE #117

If I'm not balls deep in a wife in the next few minutes, I'm going to turn into a fucking pumpkin.

—ISSUE #122

So that's it?! Wam-bam thank you, Negan?! I don't even get a sad eye-contactless hand job?!

—ISSUE #149

I didn't mean to creep you out. I mean... "love" is a strong fucking word, y'know? All I meant was... damn, girl, I've seen a lot of attractive women in my day, and I go for all kinds... *all kinds.* But this bald thing... *shit*... it's really working for me.

—ISSUE #155

I'm hoping you find me panty-drenchingly-rugged-as-fuck *handsome.* Like . . . get-me-another-skin-suit-I'm-soaking-through-this-one *handsome.*

—ISSUE #155

Your mouth says "no" but your eyes say "Fuck me until your dick breaks off inside me and fuses into some kind of Barbie doll crotch."

—ISSUE #155

Sorry. Sorry. Sometimes little Negan gets control of the mix for a second or two . . . embarrasses the fuck out of me. And if I'm honest . . . it's usually a lot more than a fucking second or two, y'know?

—ISSUE #155

Last chance... You force yourself into that woman... and I'll force this knife into your dick hole! You know what? *Too fucking late already.*

—ISSUE #156

You were a badass, and you were hot as fuck. I'd have been honored for you to be the one to kill me.

—ISSUE #167

[T]hat was more rad than foot-fucking a beautiful lady's feet pressed together to form a magic *foot-vagina* made of two feet, right? *Right?!*

What? We're all going to sit here and pretend nobody's fucked a foot before? It can't just be me...

—ISSUE #168

You're old enough to know that life is just a
constant hunt for any path that leads to fucking.
Our body wants us to make babies... but we
try not to think about that part. It's gross.

— *HERE'S NEGAN!*

Still a virgin, then?

...[G]ood for you. Take your time. Make
it special... make it count. Honestly...
push it off as long as you can.

It's kind of like that whale who ate that guy's leg and
just wouldn't leave him alone after that. Is that how
the story went? Once you get the taste of human leg,
you'll go to the ends of the Earth to get more...

...and by human leg... I mean *sex.*

— *HERE'S NEGAN!*

EXPIRED CAN EXTRAVAGANZA
(from Issue #174)

Ingredients: At least one can of severely expired pork and beans; can opener

Instructions: Obtain can; open, gag at the smell; eat it anyway; vomit; continue eating.

Notes: Maybe just one more can . . .

CHEF'S SPECIAL: SPIT-ROAST DOG
(from Issue #174)

Ingredients: One dead dog; fire

Instructions: Kill a dog (sorry, pup). Skin it and gut it. Put it on a spit over some flames. Roast that shit until crispy.

Notes: Tastes awful. Have to live with yourself for killing a dog.

APPETITES

IT'S CLEAR THAT NEGAN is a big proponent of fucking and fighting, but what about feasting? Here's the menu for Negan's post-apocalyptic diner. *Bon appétit!*

RABBIT ROAST
(from Here's Negan!)

Ingredients: One unlucky bunny.

Instructions: Kill it by some means; skin and roast it; trade half for a crossbow.

Notes: Crossbows are freakin' rad.

MYSTERY MEAT
(from Here's Negan!)

Ingredients: Small game of some kind. Raccoon? Opossum? Whatever's around and kickin'.

Instructions: Shoot it (beginner's luck); skin it; flame it; consume it.

Notes: Tastes like victory.

HE MAJORED IN BADASSERY; MINORED IN FUCKING SHIT UP

By this point, we can safely say that Negan has earned his degree from the school of hard fucking knocks. Which totally explains his bleak outlook on life. Come with us as we ponder the nature of man and his many failings... through the eyes of a total asshole.

We survive, we provide security for others, we bring civilization back to this world—we're *the Saviors*. And we can't do that without *rules.* The rules are what makes everything work. No matter how small, or insignificant, the rules are to be followed. I know it may seem trivial, or even callous on my part. There's no fucking truth to that at all.

—ISSUE #105

Just so I'm absolutely crystal fucking clear. There was a clear message I wanted to convey here today. That message is... *I can be reasonable.* I can be *completely fucking reasonable.*

In fact... I fucking prefer it that way. I don't *want* to do the bad things I do. I only do them to set boundaries, to make people aware of the consequences of their actions.

—ISSUE #107

I'm thinking...and I think about how Rick fucking threatened to kill me. How he clearly hates my fucking guts...but he's out there right now like a busy fucking bee...gathering shit to give me, so I don't hurt any of the nice folks living here. He's swallowing that hatred to get shit done. That takes guts.

Then I think about you...Spencer...the guy who waited until Rick was gone, to sneak over to talk to me, to get me to do his dirty work so that he could take Rick's place.

You wanted to take over...why not just kill Rick and take the fuck over? You know why?

Because you got no guts.

—ISSUE #111

Frankly... I've just been defending myself from a bunch of ungrateful fucks most of the time. But mostly, I'm trying to *restore order*... get things back to where they *were* before *you* came along and fucked everything up. You see... I know what it *takes* for people to survive... and it's someone like *me.* Someone to keep everyone in line, to keep everyone preoccupied so they're not focused on how goddamn miserable they are. I'm saving lives.

—ISSUE #125

What did I do that was so bad? Keeping damn near seventy people alive despite the end of the fucking world? Am I being punished for the things I did to make that happen? Are you saying you haven't done anything you regretted to keep your people alive?...Nothing that would, from an outside perspective, make you look like an evil piece of shit?

—ISSUE #141

Okay, I'll admit it...when I'm scared out of my fucking mind and pissing my pants, in the *manliest* way possible, *I will lie through my fucking teeth.* If that makes me a bad person...label away, but the term I'd use is *human.*

—ISSUE #155

Protecting the weak is the whole fucking basis
for civilization. If you're not protecting the weak,
you're not *civilized.* You're fucking *animals.*

—ISSUE #156

So many fucking people...fucking *weak,* fucking *weak-ass* fucking people. Crying. Scared. Doing every-fucking-thing in their power to get themselves killed. Spineless fucks cowering in fear until they were ripped to shreds. I was *surrounded* by them. Watched them all die...so many I lost fucking count. After a while...

I just started seeing *everyone* like that. Hell, most *everyone is* like that. Dwight, those pussies at the gate—fucking running in terror. I just lost all respect for the human race. Makes it really easy to bash a man's brains in when you think it might save all his friends... especially when you think the only way his friends can be *tricked* into living is if they're made into *slaves.* You stop seeing people as humans after a while.

—ISSUE #164

I'm not making fucking excuses. I know what I did was fucking *fucked* up one side and fucked up right back down the other. *You* helped me see that. You helped me see another way. That's why I sat in your cell. That's why I brought you Alpha's head. That's why I just *saved your fucking life.*

—ISSUE #164

After a while, after the *nerves* wore off...After I got used to the things I did...After it all started seeming *normal*...I even enjoyed it. I'll admit it. So many people died around me, right in front of me, in the early days...I started seeing everyone as living on *borrowed time,* like they were *dead already*...still up and walking around. Killing a few here and there to ensure ten or twenty people I knew, at least half of which I actually *liked*, could live? *Easy trade.*

It wasn't until Rick showed me the way...that we could actually make this world better...that we didn't have to race to the bottom of what humanity could be in order to survive...that I started to realize what I'd done.

—ISSUE #174

You're bit?! *Fuck you!* Go fucking fuck yourself up your fucking ass, you fuck. I'm *sick to death* of this shit! You ran and let your father die. You fucking flipped your shit in there . . . and let your fucking brother die, and for all your trouble . . . you get to fucking die.

I'm sick of you people. You're all fucking *weak. All you ever do is die.*

So go *die.*

—HERE'S NEGAN!

Don't bother. They last more than a few days . . . I'll learn their names. If they don't what's the point?

Nice to meet all of you. Carry on with whatever you were doing.

—HERE'S NEGAN!

Listen, *asshole.* I greeted you with a smile and you
pointed a fucking gun at me. We have guns, too...
but we don't aim them at the living. Trust me on *that.*

—HERE'S NEGAN!

I was surrounded by the dead...and survivors.
"Survivors"...that wasn't something they stayed...not
for any length of time. Never actually *earned* that title,
you feel me? Truth is, I met nothing but a long line of
people who couldn't push things just a little bit harder for
those they loved. They cracked. People died. They died.

Weak people...scared people. Maybe people like
you. I don't know yet. We're going to find out.

—HERE'S NEGAN!

I have to say, I have a *real* fucking problem
with it, too. I know what it's like to have
loved a woman, emphasis on *loved*.

You lost someone close to you? Even if you
haven't, you should still be aware of the fucking
world around you—it's *us against them,* right?
So shouldn't we try to treat us a little better?
If you'll do that with a woman . . . well maybe
you're a little closer to *them* than I'd like.

I mean, you either value a human life or you fucking
don't, right? Whatever you guys were doing . . .
it stops *now.* Or this is where we part ways.

—HERE'S NEGAN!

ISSUE BY FUCKING ISSUE

100: ||||| ||||| ||||| ||||| ||||| ||||| ||||| ||||| |||	**117:** ||||| ||||| ||||| ||||| ||||| ||||| ||||| ||||| |||||	
103: ||||| ||||| |||	**119:** ||||| ||
104: |||||	**120:** ||||| ||||| ||||| |||||	
105: ||||| ||||| ||||| ||||| ||||| |||||		**121:** ||||| ||||| ||
106: |||||		**122:** ||||| ||||| |||
107: ||||| ||||| ||||| ||||| ||||| ||	**123:** ||||| ||||| ||||| ||||| ||||
108: |||	**124:** ||||| ||||| |||||
111: ||||| ||||| ||||| ||||	**125:** ||||| ||||| ||||| ||||| ||||
112: ||||| ||||| ||||| ||||| ||||| |||||	**126:**	
113: ||||| ||||| ||||| ||||| ||||| ||||	**127:** ✕
114: ||||| ||||| ||||| ||||| |||||		**128:** ||
115: |||||	**129:**	
116: ||||| ||||| ||||| ||||	**130:** ✕

At the time of writing, Negan has appeared in fifty issues of
The Walking Dead plus one graphic novel collection, *Here's Negan!*
Here we break down, issue by issue, the man's abundant F-bombs
to discover which episodes are the most—and least—fucktastic.

140: 卌 (1)	**161:** 卌 (1)
141: 卌 卌 卌 卌 卌 ‖	**162:** ‖‖
149: 卌 卌 卌 卌	**163:** ‖‖‖
150: ✕	**164:** 卌 卌 卌 卌 卌
151: ✕	**165:** 卌
152: 卌 ‖	**166:** ‖‖‖‖
153: 卌 卌 ‖‖	**167:** ‖
154: 卌 卌 卌 卌 卌 卌 卌	**168:** 卌 卌 卌 卌 卌 卌 卌 卌 ‖
155: 卌 卌	**169:** ‖‖
156: 卌 卌 卌 卌 卌 卌 卌 ‖	**170:** ‖‖‖
157: ‖	**174:** 卌 卌 卌 卌 卌 卌
158: 卌 卌 ‖‖	***Here's Negan!*:** 卌 卌 卌 卌 卌 卌
159: 卌 卌 卌 ‖	卌 卌 卌 卌 卌 卌 卌 ‖

ACKNOWLEDGMENTS

We'd like to extend special thanks to the following folks for helping make this book a reality:

Charlie Adlard, Cliff Rathburn, Stefano Gaudiano, and the myriad other talented bastards who have worked on the comic to make Negan come to life on the page. Jeffrey Dean Morgan for playing it simultaneously charming and terrifying as fuck. Jhanteigh Kupihea, Peter Borland, Dana Sloan, Kimberly Goldstein, Paul Olsewski, Ariele Fredman, Albert Tang, Loan Le, and the rest of the team from Atria Books for kicking ass at the whole publishing thing. David Alpert and Jon Goldman for the business savvy. Sean Mackiewicz and Mike Braff for editorial oversight. Shawn Kirkham, Ross Stracke, Brian Mitchell, Ian Start, Caitlyn Brisbin, and Montana Sagnelli for the incredible cover photo shoot, and Andres Juarez for the badass cover design. Interns Sarah De Leon, Peter Holmstrom, Nicolas Saenz, and Shaily Yashar for crunching the numbers.

And, finally, thank YOU, reader, for loving Negan enough to want to read an entire fucking book about this psychopath. You fucking rock.

ABOUT THE AUTHOR

First and foremost a comic creator, Robert Kirkman has seen groundbreaking success in the adaptation of his comic books into major franchises in all forms of media, including *The Walking Dead*, *Outcast by Kirkman & Azaceta*, *Invincible*, and *Super Dinosaur*. In 2010, his Eisner Award–winning comic, *The Walking Dead*, was developed into an AMC television series, and went on to become a worldwide phenomenon. Beyond the comic world, Kirkman serves as creator, writer, and executive producer of several television shows, including *Robert Kirkman's Secret History of Comics* and *Outcast*, which is based on his popular comic book series. He lives in Los Angeles with his awesome wife and children.